# The Money Habit

## Daily Practices for Financial Success

George K. Salour

# Disclaimer

The information provided in this book is for general informational purposes only and is not intended to be, and should not be taken as, financial, investment, or legal advice. The author and publisher of this book are not financial advisors and do not endorse or recommend any particular investment or financial strategy.

Investing involves risk, including the risk of loss. The value of your investments may fluctuate and you may lose money. Past performance is not indicative of future results. It is important to carefully consider your financial goals, risk tolerance, and other personal factors before making any investment decisions.

You should consult with a financial professional before making any investment decisions and carefully review all relevant documents, including prospectuses, before investing. The author and publisher of this book are not responsible for any errors or omissions, or for any actions taken based on the information contained in this book.

This book is not a substitute for professional financial advice and should not be relied upon as such. The author and publisher of this book do not guarantee the accuracy, completeness, or usefulness of the information contained in this book and will not be liable for any errors or omissions, or for any actions taken based on the information contained in this book.

# Contents

# Chapter 1

## 1.1: The Importance of Financial Literacy

Imagine for a moment, if you will, a world where money grows on trees. You saunter out to your backyard every morning, pluck a few bills, maybe a golden coin or two, from your personal cash crop, and go about your day without a worry in the world. Sounds terrific, right? Unfortunately, as you and I well know, reality isn't quite so verdant. Money doesn't grow on trees, and acquiring it involves more than a leisurely stroll through the orchard.

In our world, the world where we're required to earn, save, spend, and invest money, being financially literate is a non-negotiable skill. And just like any other language, learning the language of money requires dedication, patience, and practice.

Financial literacy encompasses understanding how money works: how to earn it, how to manage it, how to invest it, and importantly, how to not lose it. It involves comprehension of fundamental financial principles like interest rates, compounding, inflation, risk and return, the time value of money, and the difference between stocks, bonds, mutual funds, and other investment vehicles.

It's a world where 2+2 doesn't always equal 4. It can equal 22 if you've made a wise investment or -2 if you've been a tad reckless. Financial literacy allows you to navigate this peculiar arithmetic, to emerge victorious from the trials and tribulations of tax season, to not falter in the face of fluctuating markets, and to have an answer when your credit card asks, "Will you be my Valentine?"

Having a solid grasp on financial literacy is the cornerstone to making informed decisions about money. It's about grasping how to handle debt, how to calculate interest, and how to take advantage of tax breaks. It's about appreciating the difference between good debt and bad debt, between an asset and a liability, and between diversifying your investment portfolio and putting all your eggs in one basket.

Becoming financially literate is akin to having a secret decoder ring for the world of finance. Without it, you're simply guessing, and let me tell you, guessing rarely ends well in money matters. With financial literacy, you empower yourself to build wealth, remain debt-free, and achieve financial security. So, while money might not grow on trees, understanding it can still lead to a forest of opportunity.

## 1.2: The Role of Daily Habits in Financial Success

Think of any successful person you admire, be it Warren Buffett, Serena Williams, or Bob the baker who makes the most divine croissants at the corner bakery. All these individuals have one thing in common - they're creatures of habit. And these habits, my friends, play a critical role in achieving financial success.

Contrary to popular belief, financial success isn't about hitting the jackpot in a lottery or suddenly finding a pot of gold at the end of a rainbow (though it wouldn't hurt if you did). It's more about the slow and steady accumulation of wealth over time, much like a snowball gathering mass as it rolls down a snowy hill. And this accumulation process is driven by the habits you practice day in and day out.

Daily financial habits are the small, consistent actions you take each day that contribute to your overall financial health. They're like the tiny gears in a grand old clock, often overlooked, but crucial for the entire mechanism to function smoothly.

Take budgeting, for instance. Checking your expenditure against your budget may seem like a tedious task, but done regularly, it helps ensure you live within your means and keeps impulsive purchases at bay. It's like going to the gym - one day won't make much difference, but done daily, you'll see yourself transform.

Or consider saving. Dropping a few coins into a piggy bank might feel insignificant in the moment, but when done consistently, you'll be surprised at how quickly it can add up to a significant nest egg. Remember, Rome wasn't built in a day, and neither will your bank account.

Another crucial daily habit is learning. Spend time each day to increase your financial knowledge. Be it reading a book, an article, or listening to a podcast, increasing your knowledge will help you make better financial decisions. After all, an investment in knowledge pays the best interest.

Daily habits are like financial superpowers. They might not seem flashy or impressive at first, but they pack a powerful punch in the long run. The beauty of these habits is that they don't require a lot of time or monumental effort. A few minutes each day can lead to a fortune tomorrow. So, get started on developing your daily money habits. Remember, every journey begins with a single step, or in this case, a single cent.

# 1.3: Building a New Perspective on Money

Have you ever tried on a pair of color-changing sunglasses? The world looks one way when you first put them on. But after a while, as the lenses adjust to the light, the world around you changes colors. It's still the same world, but you're seeing it differently. The same can happen when you shift your perspective about money.

When it comes to money, most of us have grown up with certain beliefs, certain ways of viewing it. It could be viewing money as a scarce resource, something hard to come by, or viewing money as the root of all evil. Some of us might view money as a means to flaunt wealth and gain social status, while others might see it as a way to provide security and comfort. Our attitudes and beliefs about money are deeply ingrained, often shaped by our upbringing, societal norms, and past experiences.

However, to achieve financial success, it's critical that we reassess these beliefs and possibly adopt a new perspective on money.

Let's think of money as a tool, not unlike a Swiss Army knife. Just as a Swiss Army knife can be used to open a can, cut a wire, or even uncork a wine bottle, money too can serve multiple purposes. It can provide for our basic needs, afford us comforts, create opportunities for experiences, provide a safety net for emergencies, and enable us to help others. When we start seeing money as a versatile tool, we can start to use it more effectively.

It's also important to understand that money in itself holds no value. It's just paper and metal, after all. The value of money lies in what it can do, what it can provide, and the freedom and options it can offer. It's a means to an end, not an end in itself.

Furthermore, recognize that having money is not a sign of greed or vanity, nor is it something to feel guilty about. It's simply a resource that you've rightfully earned and are entitled to use to enrich your life and the lives of those around you.

In the end, building a new perspective on money is like cleaning your glasses – it removes the dirt and grime clouding your vision and helps you see clearly. When you alter your viewpoint, money becomes less of a stress-inducing monster and more of a friendly ally in your journey towards financial success. It's the same money, but you're seeing it in a new light.

# 1.4: Overview of The Money Habit

Welcome to the Disneyland of money management – "The Money Habit" – where we unravel the magic formula for achieving financial success. Only here, there's no fairy godmother waving a wand. Instead, we rely on practical, achievable daily habits, financial knowledge, and a healthy mindset.

"The Money Habit" isn't just another finance book that throws jargons at you faster than a champion tennis player serves aces. It's a guide, a friend, and a mentor, helping you navigate the labyrinth of personal finance, all while making it as enjoyable as a stroll in the park. We believe in laughter, engaging stories, and the power of simplicity.

In the upcoming chapters, we'll journey together through the key areas of personal finance – mindset, budgeting, saving, investing, debt management, income diversification, retirement planning, estate planning, and even giving back. At each juncture, we'll explore how daily habits can help you master these areas, leading you to financial success.

We'll start by understanding and changing your money mindset, since your beliefs about money can either make it rain dollars or cause a drought in your bank account. Next, we'll jump into budgeting, where we make peace with our income and expenses, followed by the art of saving and the thrill of investing.

Debt management comes next, offering insights into how you can break free from the chains of debt. Income diversification, retirement, and estate planning follow suit, helping you secure your present and future. We'll wrap up with philanthropy, because what good is wealth if we can't use it to make the world a better place?

Each chapter is sprinkled with case studies that bring the concepts to life, offering you a glimpse into how real people, much like yourself, have found their path to financial success.

Buckle up and get ready for a thrilling ride through the world of personal finance. The journey will be exciting, rewarding, and sometimes challenging, but hey, as they say, "it's not about the destination, it's about the journey." And this journey, dear reader, is all set to change your life, one penny at a time.

# Chapter 2

## 2.1: Understanding Your Money Mindset

Let's begin this chapter with a quick experiment. Grab a piece of paper, and quickly write down the first five words or phrases that come to your mind when you hear the word "money." Done? Great!

Now, look at your list. Do the words lean towards the positive, like 'freedom', 'security', or 'opportunity'? Or are they more negative, such as 'stress', 'scarcity', or 'unattainable'? The way you think about money, dear reader, is your money mindset.

Your money mindset is like the glasses through which you see your financial world. It influences your attitudes towards earning, spending, saving, and investing money. It's like the director of a movie, subtly influencing the script, the actors' performances, and the final cinematic experience.

People typically have one of two basic money mindsets: a scarcity mindset or an abundance mindset.

If you're in the scarcity camp, you view money as a finite resource. You believe there's never enough to go around, and you need to fiercely guard what you have. You're like a squirrel hoarding nuts for a long winter, wary of spending or investing, worried about losing your precious stash.

On the other hand, if you have an abundance mindset, you believe there's plenty of wealth to go around. You view money as a replenishable resource and are open to spending and investing to create more wealth. You're more like a confident gardener, sowing seeds, and expecting a bountiful harvest.

Understanding your money mindset is the first step towards improving your financial health. It's like diagnosing a condition before a doctor prescribes a treatment. This introspection will help you identify unhealthy beliefs and attitudes towards money, which may be holding you back from achieving your financial goals.

So, what's your money mindset? Is it helping you, or is it behaving like that naughty kid at the back of the class, causing mischief and hindering your progress? Remember, it's never too late to change your mindset, and we're here to help you do just that. So let's roll up our sleeves and dive in!

## 2.2: How to Change Your Money Mindset

Now that we've recognized our current money mindset, it's time to roll up our sleeves and work on altering it if needed. Changing your money mindset is like learning to drive a manual transmission car after years of driving automatic. At first, it might feel awkward, even impossible, but with time and practice, it becomes second nature.

First off, identify any negative beliefs about money that you may have. Do you believe that money is evil or that it can't buy happiness? Do you think that you're destined to live paycheck to paycheck? Take these beliefs, and challenge them. Money is not inherently evil, and while it may not buy happiness, it can certainly provide the means to a comfortable life and the ability to pursue your passions.

Once you've identified these harmful beliefs, start replacing them with positive ones. This is the mental equivalent of swapping out old, worn-out parts from a car and replacing them with new, efficient ones. For instance, replace "I'll never be rich" with "I have the power to build wealth". Remind yourself that building wealth is a process, and every big fortune started with a single dollar.

Visualization can be a powerful tool in changing your money mindset. Just as athletes visualize their performance to enhance their game, you can visualize your financial success. Imagine living a life free from financial stress, where you can afford the things you need and desire. Visualize your savings account growing, your debts shrinking, and your investments yielding returns. The more vivid your visualization, the more potent its impact.

Another key to changing your money mindset is to educate yourself about money. Often, negative beliefs about money stem from a lack of understanding. Start reading books about personal finance, listen to podcasts, or attend workshops. Gaining knowledge about money will help you feel more in control and allow you to make informed decisions.

Lastly, surround yourself with positive influences. Jim Rohn, the famous motivational speaker, once said, "You are the average of the five people you spend the most time with." If you're surrounded by people who have an unhealthy relationship with money, chances are you will too. Try to be around those who handle their finances well. Their habits, attitudes, and wisdom can rub off on you.

Changing your money mindset won't happen overnight. It's like trying to lose weight - you won't see results immediately, but with consistent effort, you'll see a transformation over time. A positive money mindset is your ticket to financial success. So, fasten your seat belts and prepare for an exciting journey towards a healthier financial future.

# 2.3: Mindset Traps to Avoid

Imagine you're navigating through a dense forest. Your positive money mindset is your compass, guiding you towards financial success. But just as a forest can have traps and pitfalls, so does the path to a healthy money mindset. Here, we'll uncover some common mindset traps and how you can avoid them.

The first trap is the "I'm not a math person" belief. Some people believe that because they're not good at math, they can't handle their personal finances. It's like saying because you can't run a marathon, you shouldn't even walk around the block. You don't need to be a math wizard to manage your money well. Basic addition, subtraction, and percentages are often all you need. So, don't let your perceived math skills stand in the way of your financial well-being.

The second trap is the "Rich people are greedy" stereotype. It's a belief that can hinder your wealth-building journey, as nobody wants to be tagged as greedy. The truth is, rich people come in all types, just like any other group. There are greedy rich people, but there are also generous, kind, and humble rich people. Wealth in itself doesn't make you greedy; it merely amplifies who you already are.

Next is the "It's too late" trap. Some people believe that if they haven't started saving or investing early in life, it's too late now. But remember, it's better late than never. Just as you can plant a tree today and enjoy its shade years later, you can start working on your finances at any age and still make significant progress.

Another common trap is the "Money is the root of all problems" belief. This mindset can prevent you from seeking to earn more and save more because who wants more problems, right? The reality is, not having enough money to meet your needs and wants can be the cause of problems. When managed properly, money can provide solutions, offer security, and open up opportunities.

The final trap is the "Lack of worthiness." Some people subconsciously believe that they aren't worthy of having a lot of money. If you feel this way, remind yourself that you, like everyone else, deserve financial stability and freedom. Your worth is not defined by your bank balance.

Being aware of these mindset traps is like having a map of the forest - it shows you where the pitfalls are so you can avoid them. Always remember, your mindset is a significant factor in your financial journey. Make sure it's tuned towards abundance and success, not scarcity and failure. The right mindset, coupled with action, is your secret weapon for financial success. So, steer clear of these traps and keep moving towards your financial goals.

## 2.4: Case Studies: Mindset Shifts and Financial Success

Our journey in the world of mindsets won't be complete without some real-life tales. So, let's delve into a few stories where mindset shifts paved the way to financial success.

First, we have Maria, a single mother working two jobs to keep her family afloat. She believed that money was a scarce resource, always out of reach. One day, she stumbled upon a personal finance book at a thrift store and decided to give it a read. As she turned the pages, she began to question her scarcity mindset. She realized that she could make her money work for her rather than constantly chasing it. She started saving small amounts from her paychecks and learned to budget and invest. Today, Maria owns a small business and has a comfortable nest egg for retirement. Her life changed when she changed her money mindset.

Next, meet Kevin, a successful lawyer with a six-figure salary. Despite his high income, he was always in debt. He lived a lavish lifestyle, believing that his worth was tied to his possessions. After a serious health scare, Kevin realized the folly of his ways. He began to see money as a tool for creating a quality life rather than a measure of his self-worth. He downsized his lifestyle, paid off his debts, and started investing in his health and experiences rather than material things. Kevin's story shows that a healthy money mindset is not about how much you earn but how you manage what you earn.

Lastly, let's talk about Ruth, a retiree who believed it was too late for her to improve her financial situation. She lived on a meager pension and was afraid of outliving her savings. Her turning point came when she attended a community financial literacy workshop. She learned that it was never too late to start. With the help of a financial advisor, she invested in income-generating assets and even started a small home-based business. Today, Ruth enjoys a comfortable retirement and is a vocal advocate for financial literacy in her community.

These stories underscore that changing your money mindset can be the catalyst for financial success. Whether it's moving from a scarcity to an abundance mindset, realizing that self-worth isn't tied to possessions, or understanding that it's never too late to start, a positive shift in mindset can be a game-changer. As we leave the realm of mindset and move on to our next topic, remember - the state of your mind plays a crucial role in the state of your finances. So, keep it tuned to the frequency of abundance, prosperity, and success!

# Chapter 3

## 3.1: The Power of a Budget

In a world of debit cards, online banking, and digital currencies, money can seem a bit abstract. It comes in, it goes out, and sometimes it feels like you need to be a magician to keep it around. This is where budgeting enters the stage. Think of it as the blueprint for your financial house.

A budget helps you see your money clearly, perhaps for the first time ever. It shows you where your money comes from, where it goes, and how much (or how little) is left at the end. It's like turning on the lights in a room after fumbling in the dark.

Creating a budget gives you control over your money, rather than your money controlling you. It's like holding the reins of a horse instead of letting the horse run wild. With a budget, you dictate where your money should go instead of wondering where it went.

A budget also helps you reach your financial goals. Want to save for a house, pay off debt, or plan a dream vacation? A budget is your financial GPS, guiding you towards your destination. Without it, your financial goals are like stars in the sky – beautiful to look at but hard to reach.

Moreover, a budget can bring peace of mind. Knowing that you have a plan for your money reduces stress and eliminates financial surprises. It's like having a well-stocked pantry when a snowstorm hits – you know you're prepared.

Finally, budgeting can improve your money habits. It encourages saving, reduces impulsive spending, and makes you think twice before purchasing that fifth pair of sneakers or that flashy new gadget. It's like a personal trainer, pushing you to flex your financial discipline muscles.

Despite these benefits, many people view budgeting as restrictive – a financial diet that cuts out all the fun. But in reality, a budget doesn't limit your freedom; it gives you freedom. It's the financial equivalent of a healthy eating plan that includes both salads and occasional ice creams.

A budget is not about depriving yourself. It's about understanding your income and expenses and making conscious decisions about where you want your money to go. It's one of the most effective tools for building a strong financial future. So, ready to harness the power of a budget? Let's jump right into it!

## 3.2: How to Create a Realistic Budget

Creating a budget might seem like a daunting task, but fear not, dear reader. It's like building a Lego set. At first, all you see is a pile of bricks, but once you follow the instructions, a beautiful structure emerges.

Step one is gathering your tools. For your budget, these tools include your income details, expenses, and a medium to create your budget. This medium could be a good old pen and paper, a spreadsheet, or a budgeting app.

The next step is calculating your total income. This is the money you receive after taxes, also known as your net income. Include all sources of income like your salary, rental income, or side hustle earnings. This is like determining the size of your Lego baseplate - it sets the boundaries for your construction.

After determining your income, list all your expenses. Start with fixed expenses - these are costs that stay the same each month, such as rent or mortgage payments, utilities, and loan repayments. Next, identify your variable expenses, which change from month to month, like groceries, entertainment, and transportation. Be sure to also include non-monthly expenses such as annual insurance premiums or car maintenance. It's like sorting your Lego bricks by size and color before starting your build.

Once you have your income and expenses laid out, subtract your total expenses from your total income. If you have money left over, great! That's a surplus you can put towards savings or debt repayment. If you're in the negative, don't fret. It simply means you need to adjust your expenses, increase your income, or a combination of both.

The key to a successful budget is making it realistic. If you love dining out, don't cut it out completely – just allocate a sensible amount towards it. If you love shopping, budget for it. A budget that takes into account your lifestyle and preferences is more likely to succeed, just as a Lego set that appeals to your interests is more enjoyable to build.

Your budget is a living, breathing entity. It will need adjustments and revisions, especially in the initial months as you understand your spending patterns better. Don't be disheartened if you go over budget in some areas. It's like a Lego construction - sometimes you need to dismantle and rebuild a section to make it work.

A well-planned budget is your roadmap to financial success. It's your personal money plan, aligning your income with your expenses and financial goals. So, grab those tools and start building your financial future, one dollar at a time!

# 3.3: Maintaining Your Budget

Creating a budget is akin to making a resolution at the start of the New Year - filled with good intentions and high spirits. But, just like those well-intentioned resolutions, a budget can fall by the wayside if not regularly maintained. Think of it as a garden - you can't just plant seeds and hope for the best; you have to water, weed, and nurture those plants. Let's dive into how you can tend to your budget to ensure it grows into a lush landscape of financial stability.

Regularly tracking your spending is the first step in maintaining your budget. It's the equivalent of keeping a close eye on those budding plants for signs of trouble. Monitoring where your money goes can help you spot unnecessary expenses and adjust your budget as needed. There are numerous budgeting apps that can automate this task, or you can go old-school with a dedicated notebook or spreadsheet.

It's also important to review and adjust your budget regularly. Like seasons changing in a garden, life changes too. Maybe you got a raise (hooray!), or maybe your rent went up (boo!). Such changes will affect your budget, requiring adjustments to keep it accurate and relevant. A good rule of thumb is to review your budget every month, especially when you're starting, then perhaps every quarter once you've got the hang of it.

When maintaining your budget, be sure to accommodate for fun. A budget without any room for enjoyment is like a garden without flowers - functional, but not very uplifting. Whether it's a regular night out, a Netflix subscription, or a new gadget you've been eyeing, budgeting for fun ensures you enjoy your money while staying within your financial boundaries.

Another key aspect of maintaining your budget is setting and working towards financial goals. Want to save for a vacation? Planning to buy a house? Aim to pay off your student loans? Including these goals in your budget gives you a concrete target to work towards. It's like planting a fruit tree in your garden - it requires effort and patience, but the rewards are well worth it.

Maintaining a budget isn't about penny-pinching or deprivation. It's about making informed decisions about your money. It empowers you to control your finances instead of your finances controlling you. And with regular maintenance, what started as a simple budget can grow into a strong financial plan that supports your lifestyle and goals. Just like a well-tended garden, it will bring you both peace and prosperity. So, put on those gardening gloves and start tending to your budget!

## 3.4: Case Studies: Transformations Through Budgeting

To truly appreciate the magic of budgeting, let's delve into some real-life transformations made possible through the diligent use of this financial tool. These are not tales of lottery wins or inheritance windfalls, but stories of ordinary individuals achieving extraordinary financial stability through the power of budgeting.

First, meet Sarah. As a recent college graduate, Sarah started her first job with a hefty student loan looming over her. Despite a decent salary, she found herself living paycheck to paycheck, barely making a dent in her debt. Realizing she needed to take control of her finances, Sarah created a realistic budget, allocating a significant portion towards her loan repayment while still allowing for occasional treats. After sticking to her budget for several years, Sarah not only paid off her student loan but also saved enough for a down payment on a small apartment.

Next, we have the story of Amit and Priya, a couple with two kids. With a mortgage, car loans, and education expenses, the couple found their debt spiraling out of control. The turning point came when they received a foreclosure notice for their home. Determined to get back on track, Amit and Priya developed a strict budget, cutting back on non-essentials and negotiating lower rates on their loans. With the clarity provided by their budget, they managed to pay off their debts and save their home.

Lastly, let's visit the journey of Steve, a small business owner. With fluctuating income, Steve often found himself dipping into his savings to cover expenses during lean months. Frustrated, he decided to implement a budget, separating his business and personal expenses. He started paying himself a regular "salary" from his business income, smoothing out the fluctuations. With better control over his finances, Steve's business thrived, and his personal savings grew.

These stories illustrate the transformational power of budgeting. Regardless of the amount you earn or your financial obligations, a well-planned budget can guide you towards stability and prosperity. It's not about restricting your spending but directing your money towards your goals. As we transition to our next chapter, let's carry forward this valuable lesson: A budget is not a financial shackle, but a compass leading towards financial freedom.

# Chapter 4

## 4.1: Why Saving Matters

Imagine being invited to a masquerade ball - a dazzling event with gowns, masks, and a feast that could rival a royal banquet. Now imagine realizing you forgot your mask. The horror, right? You'd feel out of place and probably would have a less than stellar time. In a way, not having a savings plan is like forgetting your mask. You might get by, but you'd be missing out on the full experience.

Savings are crucial for numerous reasons. First off, they provide a financial safety net. Unexpected expenses are as unpredictable as a cat on a keyboard, from emergency medical costs to sudden car repairs. Having a fund set aside for such scenarios brings financial security, minimizing the impact of these unforeseen costs on your daily life. It's like carrying an umbrella in your bag - you may not need it, but it's reassuring to know it's there if the sky decides to weep.

Additionally, savings enable you to make significant purchases or investments without resorting to credit. Whether it's buying a home, starting a business, or splurging on a dream vacation, having a substantial amount saved up allows you to make these moves without plunging into debt. It's like buying a VIP pass to skip the line - it might cost more upfront, but it saves you time (and in this case, interest) in the long run.

Furthermore, saving money can lead to wealth accumulation. When combined with the power of compound interest - a magical force that makes your money multiply like rabbits - consistent savings can grow into a considerable sum over time. Think of it as planting a tiny seed that grows into a mighty oak.

Finally, saving provides peace of mind. Knowing you have money tucked away relieves financial stress and fosters a sense of achievement. Each time you add to your savings, it's like adding another book to your shelf, building towards an impressive library of financial stability.

In essence, saving is more than just stashing away money. It's an integral part of a healthy financial lifestyle, a buffer against life's curveballs, and a path towards accomplishing your financial goals. So put on that masquerade mask of savings, and let's dance our way to financial success!

## 4.2: Setting and Achieving Saving Goals

Embarking on a savings journey without clear goals is like setting sail without a destination. Sure, you'll end up somewhere, but will it be where you wanted to go? Here's your guide to setting and achieving savings goals, enabling your finances to set sail towards sunny shores.

The first step to setting savings goals is identifying what you're saving for. These goals can be short-term (like buying a new gadget), mid-term (like a down payment for a car), or long-term (like retirement). It's like marking your destinations on a map - you can have multiple places you want to visit, but you need to know where they are to plan your route.

Once you have your goals in mind, it's time to determine how much you need to save and by when. Be as precise as possible. For instance, instead of a vague goal like "Save money for a vacation," aim for "Save $3,000 for a vacation by December." This specificity provides a clear target, making your goal more tangible.

Next, create a savings plan. Determine how much you need to save each week or month to reach your goal by your desired date. It's like charting your course - you know your starting point, destination, and timeline, and now you need to plan your journey.

After setting your goals and creating your plan, it's time to start saving. Consider setting up automatic transfers to your savings account to make the process effortless. It's like having a trusty autopilot feature on your boat - you set the course, and it does the steering.

Monitor your progress regularly. If you're falling behind, consider adjusting your budget or finding ways to boost your income. If you're ahead, well, give yourself a pat on the back!

Celebrate your milestones along the way. If you've saved 50% of your goal, do a little victory dance or treat yourself (within budget, of course!). Celebrations make the journey enjoyable and motivate you to keep going.

Achieving saving goals is not a sprint but a marathon. It requires patience, discipline, and consistency. But with clear goals, a solid plan, and a dash of determination, you can navigate your finances towards your desired destinations. So hoist that sail, dear reader, and embark on your savings voyage!

# 4.3: Innovative Saving Techniques

Just as there's more than one way to peel a potato, there are myriad techniques to save money. While some may prefer the traditional cut-and-dry method of setting aside a fixed amount each month, others might find that a bit like watching paint dry. If you belong to the latter group, buckle up as we explore some innovative saving techniques that add a dash of spice to the otherwise bland task of saving money.

First on our list is the "52-Week Challenge." This is a gradual savings technique where you save $1 in the first week of the year, $2 in the second, and so on, until you're saving $52 in the last week. At the end of the year, you'll have a tidy sum of $1,378. It's a bit like playing a video game - the difficulty ramps up as you progress, but so do the rewards!

Next, we have the "No-Spend Challenge." The idea is to pick a certain period (a day, week, or month) during which you don't spend money on anything but the absolute essentials. It's like going on a financial diet, cutting out all the 'junk food' from your spending habits.

Then there's the "Round-Up Technique." Many banks and budgeting apps offer a feature where your purchases are rounded up to the nearest dollar, and the difference is transferred to your savings account. If you buy a coffee for $4.75, for instance, your account gets charged $5, and 25 cents goes to your savings. It might seem like pocket change, but it can accumulate quickly, turning your latte habit into a savings booster.

Another strategy is the "Spare Change Saving." Whenever you end up with physical coins, dump them in a jar. It's old school, yes, but you'll be amazed how much you can save without even noticing it. It's like planting a tree -

the growth is slow, but given time, you end up with something substantial.

Last but not least, there's the "Automate Your Savings" approach. With this method, you set up automatic transfers from your checking to your savings account. It's like setting a sprinkler system for your garden - once it's done, it takes care of watering without any effort from your side.

These are just a few innovative ways to make saving more interesting and less of a chore. Feel free to experiment with different techniques or even come up with your own. After all, saving money isn't a one-size-fits-all affair - it's a personal journey that's as unique as your fingerprint. So get creative, and make saving a fun and rewarding part of your financial routine!

## 4.4: Case Studies: The Impact of Saving

Weaving through the narratives of real-life savers can illuminate the transformative power of consistent saving. These are not fairy tales of money falling from the sky, but tales of everyday individuals achieving financial milestones through the power of saving.

Let's start with Lisa, a single mother working two jobs to make ends meet. Despite her tight budget, Lisa made a point to put away a small amount each week for her son's college fund. It wasn't much, maybe just the cost of a takeout meal, but over the years, those small amounts added up. By the time her son was ready for college, she had saved enough to cover his tuition for a state school.

Then, we have the tale of Mark, a young software engineer with a penchant for gadgets. Despite a comfortable salary, Mark found himself always short of cash due to his impulsive tech purchases. He decided to turn things around by setting up an automatic savings plan, diverting a portion of his paycheck to a savings account before he even had a chance to spend it. With time, not only did he build a robust emergency fund, but he also learned to control his spending and enjoy the gadgets he already owned.

Last but not least, meet Eleanor and Ben, a retired couple living on a fixed income. They cultivated the habit of saving early in their marriage, putting away a portion of their earnings into a retirement account. Over the years, with careful investments and the magic of compound interest, their modest savings grew into a substantial nest egg. In their retirement, they were able to travel, indulge in hobbies, and even set up a college fund for their grandchildren.

These stories underscore the impact saving can have on our lives. It isn't about depriving ourselves today but ensuring a more financially secure tomorrow. Whether it's securing a child's education, maintaining a comfortable lifestyle, or enjoying a worry-free retirement, the act of saving plays a critical role. It's the cushion in our financial safety net, the springboard towards our financial goals. So let's carry forward the wisdom from these tales as we chart our own financial journey: Every penny saved is a step closer to financial success.

# Chapter 5

## 5.1: Introduction to Investing

If you're thinking that investing is just for the Wolf of Wall Street types with a Ferrari and a penthouse, let me stop you right there. Investing is for everyone who wants their money to work as hard as they do. It's a way for your money to grow over time, providing a return that can help you achieve your financial goals. It's like planting a tree - you nurture it, and over time, it provides shade, fruits, and even a strong branch to hang a swing!

So, what is investing? Simply put, it's putting your money into assets such as stocks, bonds, or real estate with the expectation of generating a return or profit. Think of it as employing your money. Just as an employer expects productivity from their employees, an investor expects their investments to generate returns.

There are various types of investments, each with its own potential return and risk level. Stocks represent ownership in a company and provide a share of the company's profits through dividends or price appreciation. Bonds are like loans you give to a company or government in exchange for regular interest payments. Real estate investment could mean buying a property and earning money through rental income or selling it at a higher price.

Investing also involves understanding and managing risks. Different investments carry different levels of risk. For instance, stocks might offer high returns but come with the potential for significant price fluctuations. On the other hand, bonds are generally considered less risky, offering stable but potentially lower returns.

Keep in mind that investing isn't a get-rich-quick scheme. It requires research, patience, and sometimes a tolerance for seeing your investments go up and down. The goal isn't to make a quick buck, but to build wealth over time. Just like a game of chess, investing requires strategic thinking and patience.

Let's gear up and embark on this exciting journey of investing. It's time to put on your financial explorer hat, grab your compass of knowledge, and step into the world where money works for you!

## 5.2: How to Start Investing

Ready to start your investing journey, but not sure where to begin? It's like being at the starting line of a marathon with no clue which direction to run. Fret not! Here's a step-by-step guide to help you kick off your investing adventure.

Step one: Set clear financial goals. You need to know why you're investing. Are you saving for a house, planning for retirement, or aiming to fund a child's education? These goals will guide your investing decisions, just like a GPS guiding you on a road trip.

Step two: Educate yourself. Knowledge is your most potent weapon in investing. Understand the basics of different investment types, risk and return, diversification, and compounding. It's like learning the rules before playing a new board game.

Step three: Determine your risk tolerance. Are you comfortable with the value of your investments fluctuating? Can you handle potential losses in the short term for potentially higher gains in the long term? Answering these questions will help you choose investments that align with your comfort level. It's like deciding whether to go for a peaceful cruise or a thrilling roller-coaster ride.

Step four: Create an investment plan. Based on your goals and risk tolerance, decide how much of your portfolio should be in different types of investments. This is your asset allocation strategy. Think of it as planning a balanced diet for your finances.

Step five: Choose an investment account. This could be a retirement account like a 401(k) or an IRA, a standard brokerage account, or a robo-advisor account. It's like picking the right vehicle for your journey.

Step six: Start investing! You can buy stocks, bonds, mutual funds, ETFs, or real estate, depending on your plan. Remember, you don't need a lot of money to start investing. Many platforms allow investing with as little as $5. It's like starting a fitness routine - you don't need to run a marathon on day one, even a short jog is a good start.

Step seven: Monitor and adjust. Regularly check your portfolio and make adjustments as needed based on changes in your goals, risk tolerance, or market conditions. It's like regular health check-ups to ensure your financial fitness.

Starting to invest might seem daunting, but with clear goals, adequate knowledge, and a well-thought-out plan, you can navigate the investment landscape confidently. So, lace up your financial sneakers and get ready to run the marathon of investing!

# 5.3: Creating a Balanced Investment Portfolio

Creating a balanced investment portfolio is like cooking a well-rounded meal. You wouldn't just serve a plate full of potatoes for dinner, would you? Similarly, having a diversified portfolio helps ensure that your investments provide a mix of flavors, providing both growth and protection for your financial future.

Here's your recipe for a balanced portfolio:

Ingredient 1: Diversification. This involves spreading your investments across different asset classes such as stocks, bonds, and real estate. By doing so, you reduce the risk associated with putting all your eggs in one basket. It's akin to using different ingredients in a dish to balance out flavors and nutrition.

Ingredient 2: Asset Allocation. This refers to how much of your portfolio is invested in each type of asset. The ideal allocation depends on your risk tolerance, investment goals, and time horizon. It's like deciding how much of each ingredient to use in your recipe. A young investor with a long time horizon might have a larger portion in stocks for higher growth, while a retiree might prefer a larger portion in bonds for income and stability.

Ingredient 3: Regular Rebalancing. Over time, due to market fluctuations, your actual asset allocation may drift from your original plan. Regularly reviewing and adjusting your portfolio to bring it back to your desired allocation is essential. It's like tasting and adjusting the seasoning in your dish as you cook.

Ingredient 4: Dollar-cost averaging. This is a technique where you invest a fixed amount at regular intervals, regardless of market conditions. This approach can help reduce the impact of market volatility and avoid the risks of trying to time the market. It's similar to adding water gradually while cooking, to avoid over or under-cooking.

Ingredient 5: Patience and Discipline. The key to successful investing is to stick to your plan, avoid emotional decisions, and give your investments time to grow. Just like a dish needs time to cook, your investments need time to mature.

There's no one-size-fits-all recipe for a balanced portfolio. Each investor's situation is unique, and what works for one may not work for another. Just like each chef has their own signature style, each investor needs a personalized approach. So don your apron, roll up your sleeves, and start cooking up your balanced investment portfolio!

# 5.4: Case Studies: Success Stories in Investing

Are you ready to dive into a collection of inspiring investing tales? Each story features ordinary individuals who created extraordinary wealth through investing. Their experiences reveal the power of investing as a tool to achieve financial goals. So, grab a cup of tea (or a fancy latte, we're not judging), sit back, and let these stories inspire you.

Our first story features Maria, a high school teacher. In her early 20s, Maria started investing in low-cost index funds with a small portion of her modest salary. She stuck to her investment plan, consistently investing each month, despite market fluctuations. Thanks to the magic of compound interest, by the time Maria retired, her investment portfolio had grown to a substantial sum, allowing her to enjoy a comfortable retirement and leave a generous legacy for her family.

Next, meet John, a software developer with a passion for technology. John used his knowledge and passion to invest in tech startups. While some of his early investments didn't pan out, John struck gold when a small e-commerce company he invested in became a global giant. His initial investment multiplied manifold, transforming his financial landscape.

Finally, let's talk about Amy, a real estate agent. Amy used her expertise to invest in rental properties. She carefully selected properties in growing neighborhoods and managed them efficiently. The rental income provided a steady cash flow, while the properties appreciated in value over time, creating a profitable investment portfolio.

These stories underscore different facets of successful investing. Maria's story illustrates the power of regular investing and compound interest. John's tale emphasizes the potential rewards of investing in what you know and understand. Amy's experience underscores the importance of using your skills and expertise in your investment strategy.

Each tale is unique, but the underlying message remains the same: Investing can be a powerful tool in building wealth. Whether you're a teacher, a tech enthusiast, a real estate expert, or anything in between, there's an investment strategy that can work for you. As you venture forth in your investing journey, may these stories serve as a source of inspiration and a reminder of the power of smart, consistent investing.

# Chapter 6

## 6.1: Understanding Good and Bad Debt

When it comes to debt, it's easy to think of it as a fire-breathing dragon that's out to burn all your financial dreams. But, hold onto your knight's helmet, because not all debt is created equal. There's good debt and bad debt, just as there are friendly dragons and not-so-friendly ones.

Let's start with 'good debt.' Good debt is generally considered an investment that will grow in value or generate long-term income. Like taming a dragon to fly you to work, it can provide some long-term benefits.

For example, a mortgage is often considered good debt. As you pay off your mortgage, you build equity in a home that may appreciate in value. It's like growing your own dragon from a hatchling and watching it mature over time.

Student loans can also be good debt if they lead to a degree and better job prospects. It's like training your dragon to do tricks, enhancing its value and performance.

On the other hand, 'bad debt' refers to debt incurred to purchase things that quickly lose their value and do not generate long-term income. It's like feeding your dragon loads of expensive gourmet food that just goes up in smoke.

Credit card debt is often considered bad debt because it generally carries high interest rates, and the items purchased with credit cards (like a new pair of shoes or a gaming system) typically do not increase in value.

Similarly, a car loan can be seen as bad debt because vehicles typically depreciate quickly. It's like investing in a dragon that gets smaller and less powerful over time.

Of course, the distinction between good and bad debt isn't always clear-cut, and it depends on individual circumstances. The key is to understand the impact of debt on your financial health and make informed decisions. Just like handling dragons, it requires careful thought, planning, and a good dose of courage. Armed with this knowledge, you're well-prepared to face the fiery world of debt.

# 6.2: Strategies for Reducing Debt

Reducing debt can often feel like trying to lose weight. You know it's beneficial for your health, but it can seem challenging, especially when you're just getting started. But with the right strategy and a dollop of discipline, you can whittle down your debt like shedding those extra pounds after the holidays.

Let's explore some of the most effective debt-reduction strategies.

The Avalanche Method: This strategy involves paying off debts with the highest interest rates first while making minimum payments on other debts. Once the highest-interest debt is paid off, you move to the next highest, and so on. It's like starting your weight loss journey with the heaviest weights in the gym.

The Snowball Method: With this strategy, you start by paying off the smallest debts first, while keeping up with minimum payments on the rest. As each debt is paid off, you roll the money you were paying on that debt into the next smallest debt. It's like starting a workout regime with light exercises and gradually taking on more challenging ones.

Consolidation Loans: This involves taking out a new loan with a lower interest rate to pay off multiple debts at once. This not only simplifies your payments but can also save you money in the long run. It's akin to combining several small meals into one balanced and nutritious meal.

Balance Transfers: If you have high-interest credit card debt, you might consider transferring your balances to a card with a lower interest rate, often as a promotional offer. This can help you save on interest costs and pay off your debt faster. It's like switching from high-calorie snacks to healthier alternatives.

The 'Extra Payment' Strategy: This involves making more than the minimum payment, or making an extra payment when you can. This can significantly reduce the amount of interest you'll pay over the life of the loan. It's like adding an extra workout session to your regular routine.

Reducing debt is not a one-size-fits-all process. What worked for your friend or neighbor might not work for you. It's crucial to find a strategy that fits your financial situation and stick to it. With persistence and discipline, you can successfully trim down your debt and bolster your financial health. Now, who's ready for a financial workout?

## 6.3: How to Stay Debt-Free

So, you've slain the debt dragon, and it feels fantastic, like you've just won the lottery, found the Holy Grail, and climbed Mount Everest all at once. But now comes another challenge: staying debt-free. It's like maintaining your weight after a diet - it requires a balanced approach and commitment. Here are some tips to keep that dragon at bay.

Stick to a Budget: A budget is your financial compass, guiding you to make wise spending decisions. It can help you avoid overspending and falling back into debt. It's like having a fitness tracker - it keeps you in line and helps you stay on track.

Build an Emergency Fund: An emergency fund serves as a financial safety net, covering unexpected expenses without having to borrow money. Aim for three to six months' worth of living expenses. It's like storing nuts for the winter - you never know when you might need them.

Use Credit Wisely: Just because you have a credit card doesn't mean you have to use it for every purchase. Try to use credit sparingly and always pay off your balance in full each month to avoid interest charges. It's like having a box of chocolates - just because it's there doesn't mean you should eat them all at once.

Save for Large Purchases: Instead of borrowing money for large purchases, save up for them in advance. It may require patience, but it will save you from paying interest and potentially accumulating more debt. It's like slowly saving up pieces for a puzzle - in the end, you'll have a beautiful picture without missing any parts.

Stay Informed: Keep learning about personal finance. The more you understand about money management, the better equipped you'll be to make wise financial decisions. It's like being a lifelong learner - the more knowledge you gain, the brighter your light shines.

Staying debt-free is a journey, not a destination. It requires ongoing commitment, just like staying healthy or maintaining a garden. But with discipline and the right strategies, you can keep that debt dragon defeated and enjoy the freedom and peace of mind that comes with being debt-free. Now, who's ready for a victory dance?

# 6.4: Case Studies: Overcoming Debt

Are you ready for some real-life inspiration? We're about to delve into the stories of individuals who found themselves trapped in the dungeons of debt and, with grit, determination, and strategic planning, managed to escape to the bright light of financial freedom. So sit back, pop some popcorn, and let's get inspired!

First, meet Lisa, a single mother with a mountain of credit card debt. After her divorce, Lisa found herself using credit cards to cover basic expenses. Realizing she was sinking deeper into debt, she decided to make a change. Lisa created a strict budget, cut unnecessary expenses, and focused on paying off her high-interest debt first using the avalanche method. It was a long and arduous journey, but Lisa was determined. And eventually, she became debt-free, freeing herself and her children from the shackles of debt.

Next, there's Mike, a college graduate drowning in student loans. Mike owed a substantial amount of money, with multiple loans, each with a different interest rate. Overwhelmed, he decided to consolidate his student loans, resulting in a single monthly payment with a lower interest rate. With a more manageable repayment plan, Mike was able to gradually pay off his debt while also saving for his future.

Lastly, let's talk about Rosa and Carlos, a couple who fell into debt after buying a house they couldn't afford. The mortgage payments were suffocating, and they realized they needed to make a drastic change. They decided to downsize, selling their house and moving to a smaller, more affordable home. With the money from the sale, they paid off their original mortgage and focused on living within their means. The couple now lives debt-free and has a healthier relationship with money.

These stories highlight the power of determination, strategy, and wise financial decision-making in overcoming debt. Each journey is unique, but they all offer the same hope: escaping debt is possible, and you don't have to do it alone. Use these tales as motivation as you chart your own path to a debt-free life. You've got this!

# Chapter 7

## 7.1: The Need for Multiple Income Streams

In the wild, relying on a single food source can leave an animal vulnerable during times of scarcity. Similarly, relying solely on one income stream can make you financially vulnerable when life throws curveballs. Having multiple income streams is like having a buffet at your disposal - if one dish runs out, you still have plenty of others to feast on.

A single income stream might seem sufficient, especially if you have a well-paying job. However, as recent economic downturns have shown, job security can sometimes be as elusive as a unicorn sighting. Layoffs, health issues, or sudden market changes can disrupt your primary income, potentially leading to financial instability.

By diversifying your income streams, you create a safety net. If one source of income takes a hit, you have others to fall back on. It's like having a team of superheroes - if one can't save the day, another steps up to the plate.

Multiple income streams can also speed up your journey to financial goals. If you're trying to pay off debt, save for retirement, or amass wealth, extra income can accelerate your progress. It's like riding a high-speed train Instead of a horse-drawn carriage - you'll reach your destination faster.

Finally, multiple income streams can provide opportunities for personal growth and fulfillment. They allow you to explore different interests, develop new skills, and potentially discover new passions. It's like adding a variety of spices to your life's stew - each one brings a unique flavor and enhances the overall dish.

Now, you might be thinking, "This sounds great, but where do I start?" Don't worry, we'll cover that in the next section. For now, just remember: multiple income streams aren't just for the wealthy or business-savvy. They're for anyone looking to fortify their financial fortress, accelerate their wealth-building journey, and spice up their life with new opportunities. Who's ready to feast?

## 7.2: Ideas for Side Income

Feeling ready to diversify your income streams but not sure where to start? Consider this your idea factory for generating side income. It's like an all-you-can-eat buffet of potential money-making endeavors. So, grab a plate and let's start serving!

Freelancing: If you have a particular skill set, like writing, graphic design, programming, or marketing, you can offer your services as a freelancer. It's like being a mercenary, but instead of swinging swords, you're creating stunning logos or crafting persuasive articles.

Online Teaching or Tutoring: If you have expertise in a subject, consider sharing your knowledge online. You could teach English to foreign students, tutor high school math, or even provide piano lessons. It's like being a Jedi Master, passing your wisdom onto the next generation.

Selling Handmade Goods or Crafts: If you have a knack for making things, why not turn that hobby into a profit? You can sell anything from knitted scarves to homemade candles on platforms like Etsy. It's like being

Santa's elf, but you're making gifts for customers, not just for good boys and girls.

Renting Out Extra Space: If you have an extra room or a vacant vacation home, consider renting it out on Airbnb. It's like turning your property into a mini-hotel, without the need for those tiny shampoo bottles.

Gig Economy: Platforms like Uber, Lyft, and TaskRabbit allow you to earn money on your own schedule. Whether you're driving people around or assembling furniture, the gig economy can provide a flexible income source. It's like being a superhero for hire, ready to save the day one gig at a time.

Stock Photography: If you have a good eye and a decent camera, you can sell your photos on stock photo websites. It's like turning your world into a canvas and selling pieces of your perspective.

The key to side income is to find something that aligns with your skills, interests, and schedule. It should ideally be something you enjoy so it doesn't feel like just another job. So, dig into this buffet of ideas, and see what dish - or dishes - appeal to you most. Bon appétit!

# 7.3: How to Scale Your Side Income

Great, now you have a side hustle going! You're bringing in some extra dough and feeling like a financial chef, cooking up delicious financial gains. But what if I told you that your side hustle could be more than just a side dish? That's right, we're talking about turning your extra source of income into a main course. Grab your apron, it's time to scale up.

Reinvest in Your Business: Pouring a portion of your profits back into your side gig can supercharge its growth. This could mean investing in better equipment, upskilling through a course, or spending on marketing. It's like giving your plants high-quality fertilizer - they grow bigger and yield more fruits.

Automate and Delegate: As your side income grows, you may find repetitive tasks eating up your time. Consider using automation tools or outsourcing certain tasks. It's like having your own team of robotic assistants, handling the mundane so you can focus on the strategic.

Diversify Your Offerings: If you're selling a product or service, think about what else your customers might want. Offering complementary products or upselling premium services can boost your income. It's like being a savvy ice cream vendor who realizes they can sell cones, toppings, and even waffles alongside their ice cream.

Build a Brand: A recognizable brand can attract more customers and allow you to charge premium prices. Invest time in developing your brand's personality, visual identity, and value proposition. It's like donning a superhero costume - you become instantly recognizable and synonymous with certain values.

Expand Your Reach: Utilize online marketing strategies like SEO, social media, and email marketing to reach a wider audience. The more people know about your side hustle, the more potential customers you have. It's like casting a wider net - you'll catch more fish.

Remember, scaling up a side income requires strategic planning, patience, and consistent effort. It's like baking bread - you need the right ingredients, the right temperature, and enough time to rise. But with dedication and a dash of entrepreneurial spirit, you can turn your side income into a hearty financial feast. Let's get cooking!

# 7.4: Case Studies: Income Diversification Success

We've now explored the need for multiple income streams and provided ideas to generate and scale side income. But hey, let's bring it to life! Here are a few real-world examples of individuals who have successfully diversified their income streams and created financial buffets that would make Gordon Ramsay proud.

Our first case is Emily, a high school teacher. With her passion for baking, Emily started selling homemade cookies at local farmers' markets on weekends. As her cookies gained popularity, she reinvested her profits in professional baking equipment and created a website to accept online orders. Today, Emily's side hustle has grown into a full-blown business, and her financial life is sweeter than ever.

Next, we have Tim, a software developer with a flair for photography. He began by uploading his photos to a stock photography website. As his photos sold, he diversified by offering freelance event photography services and selling prints of his best shots on his website. Today, Tim's photography adds a beautiful lens to his income diversity.

Finally, let's meet Mia, a corporate executive who invested in a rental property. While it started as a minor source of passive income, Mia saw the potential for more. She purchased two additional properties, hired a property management company to handle day-to-day operations, and has created a robust stream of passive income.

Each of these individuals has taken their passions, skills, or investment opportunities and transformed them into substantial income streams. Their stories show that with the right approach, creativity, and hard work, income diversification isn't just possible—it's a recipe for financial success. The kitchen is open, and it's your turn to cook up your own diversified income buffet. Bon appétit!

# Chapter 8

## 8.1: Why It's Never Too Early to Plan for Retirement

Picture this: you're sipping a piña colada on a sandy beach, the sun setting over the sparkling ocean, without a worry in the world. Sounds like an ideal retirement, right? But to get there, you can't just snap your fingers at age 65 and expect it to happen. Like a master gardener growing a prize-winning rose, retirement requires careful planning, time, and nurturing.

The earlier you start planning for retirement, the better. This is not only because the magic of compound interest works best over long periods (it's like a snowball gaining speed and size as it rolls down a hill) but also because the earlier you start, the more room you have to adjust and adapt your plan.

Imagine you're setting out on a journey. The sooner you map out your route, the more time you have to prepare, identify potential roadblocks, and find alternate routes. Retirement is like that journey - and your financial plan is the roadmap.

Planning early for retirement also affords you the opportunity to take on more risk in your investment portfolio, potentially leading to higher returns over time. It's like being a young, fearless skateboarder, able to try more tricks, compared to an older, more cautious one.

Moreover, early retirement planning eases the pressure of saving huge amounts as you get closer to retirement. Rather than frantically stuffing cash under your mattress, you can make regular, manageable contributions to your retirement fund. It's like gently adding layers to a lasagna over time rather than trying to pile them on all at once.

Retirement isn't an age - it's a financial status. The sooner you start planning for it, the more likely you'll achieve the financial independence required to sip that piña colada without any worries. So, let's get planting!

# 8.2: Strategies for Effective Retirement Planning

Retirement planning can seem like a daunting task. You might feel like you're trying to assemble a thousand-piece puzzle without the picture on the box. But don't worry! I'm here with a clear image and some strategies to help you piece together your retirement plan.

Understand Your Retirement Needs: Begin by estimating how much money you'll need in retirement. Consider your desired lifestyle, potential healthcare costs, and longevity. It's like determining the amount of fuel you need for a cross-country road trip.

Start Saving Now: Don't wait until you're closer to retirement to start saving. Begin now, no matter your age, and save consistently. Every dollar saved is a step closer to your retirement goal. It's like filling your water reservoir drop by drop, eventually creating a vast lake.

Leverage Employer Retirement Plans: If your employer offers a retirement plan like a 401(k) or 403(b), make the most of it. Especially if they match your contributions – that's free money you don't want to miss out on. It's like a buy-one-get-one-free deal at your favorite store.

Diversify Your Investments: Spread your investments across different asset classes to reduce risk and increase potential returns. It's like not putting all your eggs in one basket, especially if that basket tends to wobble.

Create an Emergency Fund: Having three to six months' worth of living expenses in a readily accessible account can prevent you from dipping into your retirement savings in case of an emergency. It's like having a spare tire in your car – you hope you don't need it, but you're glad it's there when you do.

Regularly Review and Adjust Your Plan: Retirement planning isn't a set-it-and-forget-it situation. As you age, your financial situation and the economic environment will change. Regularly reviewing and adjusting your plan ensures it remains effective. It's like recalibrating your GPS during a long journey.

Retirement planning is like a marathon, not a sprint. With the right strategies and a bit of patience, you'll be crossing the finish line with your arms raised in triumph, ready to enjoy your golden years in financial comfort. On your marks, get set, go!

# 8.3: Maximizing Your Retirement Investments

You're saving for retirement and have made some investments. That's fantastic! You've planted the seeds for your retirement garden. But what if I told you we could turn that garden into a lush forest? That's right! Here are some strategies to maximize your retirement investments.

Utilize Tax-Advantaged Accounts: Take advantage of accounts like IRAs and 401(k)s, which offer tax benefits. It's like having a magic shield that guards your treasure from the tax dragon.

Contribute the Maximum: Whenever possible, aim to contribute the maximum allowed amount to your retirement accounts each year. It's like packing an extra sandwich for a hike - you'll appreciate it later.

Catch-up Contributions: If you're aged 50 or over, the IRS allows you to make additional 'catch-up' contributions to your retirement accounts. It's like being given the chance to add extra layers to your winter clothing before stepping out into the snow.

Invest in Index Funds: These funds aim to track the performance of a specific market index. They're typically low cost and remove the need to pick individual stocks, which can be risky. It's like riding in a bus with other people instead of taking a solo bike ride on a rocky path.

Consider Real Estate Investment Trusts (REITs): REITs can provide a steady stream of income and diversification benefits. It's like adding a rent-paying tenant to your forest of money trees.

Seek Professional Advice: A financial advisor can provide personalized advice based on your specific circumstances and goals. It's like having a skilled botanist helping you grow your forest.

Remember, investing for retirement isn't just about stashing away money. It's about strategically growing and safeguarding your wealth. With these strategies, your garden of retirement savings can grow into a flourishing forest, providing you with shade, sustenance, and comfort in your retirement years. Time to get growing!

# 8.4: Case Studies: Early Retirement Successes

In this world of ours, there's no shortage of people who've hustled, saved, and invested their way to early retirement. Let's take a glimpse at a few of them. Get ready for some real-life stories that could give Hollywood's best screenwriters a run for their money.

Our first success story revolves around David, a software engineer. With his keen interest in finance, David began saving a substantial portion of his salary in his mid-twenties. He maximized his contributions to his 401(k), invested in low-cost index funds, and capitalized on the power of compound interest. David also started a successful side gig building custom software for small businesses, which added another income stream. By his early forties, David retired and now spends his time volunteering and traveling the world. Talk about coding his way to early retirement!

Next up, we have Sarah, a school teacher. Sarah lived frugally and saved more than 50% of her income, which she put into a diversified investment portfolio. She also started a tutoring business on the side, funneling all the profits into her retirement fund. This "penny-wise pound richer" lifestyle allowed Sarah to retire in her early fifties, and she now spends her days indulging her passion for painting and hiking.

Lastly, let's meet Tom and Linda, a couple who ran a small restaurant. They invested in a series of rental properties in their local area, creating a steady stream of passive income. By living modestly and reinvesting the profits from their rentals, they amassed a sizeable nest egg. At 55, they sold their restaurant, retired, and are now happily spending their days spoiling their grandchildren and exploring the world one cruise at a time.

Each story is unique, yet they all share common themes: the power of saving, the importance of multiple income streams, and the incredible growth potential of smart investments. And remember, if they can do it, why not you? Your early retirement script is waiting to be written. Lights, camera, action!

# Chapter 9

## 9.1: Understanding the Importance of Estate Planning

Estate planning. Sounds like a topic only for the rich and famous, doesn't it? Like something you'd see in a period drama where a wealthy patriarch, wearing a velvet robe and puffing on a cigar, leaves his vast fortune to his favorite pet parrot. But believe it or not, it's not just for the parrot-inheriting elite. It's a crucial component of personal finance that applies to everyone.

Estate planning, at its core, is about ensuring that your assets are distributed according to your wishes after your passing. It's like being a director of your own movie, setting the stage and the script to be followed when you're no longer there.

Without a proper estate plan, you leave your assets and your loved ones at the mercy of state laws. This can result in unnecessary expenses, familial disputes, and a distribution of your assets that might not align with your wishes. It's like tossing a salad without first deciding on the ingredients - the result might be palatable, but it's not what you had in mind.

In addition, estate planning allows you to minimize taxes, making sure your heirs receive the maximum benefit from your assets. It's like packing a lunch for your children and making sure they get the biggest slice of your homemade apple pie, instead of handing over a large chunk to the school bully.

Moreover, estate planning extends beyond just physical assets. It includes directives about your healthcare and care of minor children if you're unable to make decisions. It's like writing an instruction manual for the most precious parts of your life.

Everyone leaves an estate, no matter how large or small. By planning your estate, you maintain control, provide for your loved ones, and leave a legacy that reflects your wishes. So, velvet robe or not, let's embark on this important part of your financial journey.

## 9.2: Basic Steps for Estate Planning

Estate planning may feel like you're navigating a labyrinth with its own minotaur. Fear not! Here's your Ariadne's thread, a step-by-step guide to basic estate planning that will lead you safely through.

Inventory Your Assets: Begin by listing everything you own - real estate, bank accounts, investments, retirement funds, vehicles, jewelry, even your treasured comic book collection. This is the treasure map to your estate.

Identify Your Heirs: Determine who you want to inherit your assets. This could include family, friends, charities, or even your favorite cat. Remember, this isn't a popularity contest - it's about your wishes.

Draft a Will: A will is a legal document outlining who gets what from your estate. If you don't have one, the state decides, and they probably won't give the dog your best slippers. Consider a lawyer's help to ensure all legal requirements are met.

Consider a Trust: A trust allows you to set conditions on how certain assets are distributed and can minimize estate taxes. It's like a treasure chest with a sophisticated lock.

Assign Power of Attorney: Designate someone to handle your finances and legal affairs if you're unable to do so. It's like having a reliable understudy for your financial performance.

Designate Beneficiaries: For accounts like life insurance and retirement plans, ensure you have designated beneficiaries. It's a direct ticket for these assets to reach the right person.

Create a Living Will and Healthcare Proxy: A living will expresses your wishes for end-of-life care, while a healthcare proxy designates someone to make healthcare decisions if you can't. It's like having a personal representative for your health matters.

Review Regularly: Review your estate plan regularly, especially after major life events like marriage, divorce, births, deaths, or significant changes in your assets. It's about keeping your map updated.

These are just the basics. Depending on your estate, you may need more advanced strategies. So, arm yourself with this knowledge, seek professional help if needed, and step confidently into the estate planning labyrinth. There's no minotaur here, just peace of mind and a well-organized legacy. Let's go!

# 9.3: Managing and Protecting Your Assets

In our journey through the realm of personal finance, we've arrived at the fortress where your wealth resides. Your assets. As much as acquiring assets is essential, managing and protecting them is equally crucial. But fret not, my friend, we're here to help you become a seasoned steward of your fortress.

Insurance: When it comes to defending your fortress, insurance is like your protective moat. Homeowner's insurance, auto insurance, life insurance, health insurance, disability insurance – they can shield you from financial loss and protect your assets.

Diversification: Don't store all your valuables in one room of the fortress. In the investment world, diversification is your friend. It reduces risk by spreading your investments across various financial instruments, industries, and other categories.

Asset Allocation: This is deciding what percentage of your portfolio should be invested in different asset classes (stocks, bonds, cash, etc.). It's like deciding which rooms in your fortress should hold which type of treasure – paintings, jewels, or gold bars.

Estate Planning: We've covered this already, but it's worth repeating. A good estate plan can help protect your assets from being devoured by taxes or ending up in the wrong hands.

Regular Appraisals: You wouldn't ignore a creaky door or a leaky roof in your fortress, would you? Similarly, regularly appraise your assets, especially real estate and personal valuables, to know their worth and ensure they're adequately insured.

Limiting Liability: This could mean structuring your business correctly to protect your personal assets, or simply not co-signing loans. It's like not letting potential siege armies anywhere near your fortress.

Managing and protecting your assets is an ongoing process, not a one-time event. It requires time, attention, and often professional advice. But with a well-maintained and guarded fortress, you can sleep soundly knowing your wealth is secure. And perhaps you can afford to hire a court jester for some laughs too!

# 9.4: Case Studies: Effective Estate Planning

Ahoy, financial explorers! It's time to voyage through the real world and meet some savvy navigators who've charted the waters of estate planning. Unfurl the sails, and let's set course towards our first tale.

Meet Edna, an art collector with a vibrant assortment of modern art. With the guidance of a financial advisor, Edna created a revocable living trust, assigning her daughter as the successor trustee. She transferred ownership of her art to the trust, ensuring her collection would be managed according to her wishes after her passing. This effectively avoided the long probate process, and her daughter was able to continue hosting art exhibitions, just as Edna had envisioned. A Picasso-esque victory, wouldn't you say?

Next, let's voyage to Paul, a small business owner. Paul was worried about his business's future after his retirement. He worked with an estate planning attorney to draft a comprehensive business succession plan and a living will. Today, his children run the business successfully, honoring his legacy. A fruitful sail on tumultuous seas!

Our final stop takes us to the shores of Anna, a single mother with two young children. Anna didn't have a vast estate but wanted to ensure her children would be taken care of if something happened to her. She purchased a life insurance policy, naming a trust as the beneficiary, with her sister as the trustee to manage the funds for her children's needs. It was her lighthouse, guiding her peace of mind.

Each of these stories shines a beacon on the importance of effective estate planning. Whether it's art collections, small businesses, or ensuring care for loved ones, thorough estate planning can navigate us towards calm waters. So, hoist your sails, because estate planning is an adventure where you chart the course. Safe voyaging!

# Chapter 10

## 10.1: The Role of Philanthropy in Personal Finance

In the world of personal finance, philanthropy often appears like a luxury yacht moored in the harbor. It's beautiful, it's admirable, but it feels like it belongs to someone else. But, philanthropy, my dear reader, isn't only for the ultra-wealthy. It's for anyone who wants to make a difference, and it can play a pivotal role in your financial journey.

Philanthropy is giving your resources - money, time, or skills - for the betterment of society. It's like sowing seeds in a community garden; the flowers that bloom bring joy to many. It allows you to support causes you're passionate about, be it education, health, environment, or arts.

But here's the twist. Philanthropy isn't just about giving; it's also about gaining. It enriches your life with purpose and fulfillment, but it also offers tangible financial benefits.

Donations to qualified charitable organizations can lead to tax deductions, reducing your taxable income. It's like a coupon from the government for doing good!

Strategic philanthropy can also be a valuable tool in estate planning. It can help minimize estate and inheritance taxes while ensuring your wealth benefits the causes close to your heart. It's like being a financial wizard, conjuring good deeds while reducing taxes.

In addition, philanthropy can be an opportunity to teach financial values to your children. It's like a classroom where lessons of generosity, gratitude, and fiscal responsibility come alive.

Get ready to cast off the ropes and set sail on your philanthropic journey. The luxury yacht of philanthropy is not just for someone else. It's for you, too. Happy sailing!

## 10.2: How to Integrate Giving into Your Financial Plan

Alright, dear readers, it's time to talk about how we can incorporate the elegance of the waltz, the precision of the tango, and the passion of the salsa into our financial plan. Yes, we're talking about the dance of giving!

Budget for Giving: Like setting aside funds for groceries or entertainment, allocate a portion of your income for giving. It doesn't have to be enormous – even a little can create ripples of change.

Automate Donations: Many charitable organizations offer options to automate your donations. It's like setting up a recurring dance appointment, ensuring you don't miss a beat.

Donate Appreciated Stocks: Donating stocks, particularly those that have appreciated greatly, can be a savvy move. Not only can the full market value be deductible, but you may also avoid capital gains tax. That's dancing with style!

Charitable Trusts and Foundations: If you have substantial assets, setting up a charitable trust or foundation can be beneficial. It allows you to make significant contributions while reaping potential tax benefits.

Donor-Advised Funds: Think of this as your personal fund for philanthropy. You contribute to the fund, receive a tax deduction, and then recommend grants to your chosen charities over time.

Legacy Giving: This involves integrating charitable giving into your estate planning. Bequests, charitable remainder trusts, or naming charities as beneficiaries in your retirement or insurance plans – there are many ways to dance this waltz.

Giving Time and Skills: Philanthropy isn't just about money. Volunteering your time or offering your skills can make a significant difference too.

Integrating giving into your financial plan doesn't just help others; it can also provide personal benefits and deep satisfaction. So, lace up those dancing shoes, and let's make philanthropy part of our financial dance!

## 10.3: Making a Difference Without Sacrificing Financial Stability

Roll up your sleeves, folks, because we're about to dig into the satisfying blend of benevolence and financial sense. Making a difference without sacrificing financial stability? You betcha! And here's how:

Microloans: No, these are not tiny loans for ants. Microloans are small loans given to low-income entrepreneurs and small businesses who have no access to traditional banking services. You can provide a microloan through platforms like Kiva, help someone across the world expand their business, and get your money back – it's like having your cake and eating it too!

Give Stocks: Donating appreciated stocks allows you to make a significant contribution while avoiding capital gains tax. You could also get a tax deduction. It's like the Batman of giving – sleek, smart, and strategic.

Employer Matching: Many employers match employee donations to qualified charitable organizations. This effectively doubles your donation without doubling the cost for you – a high-five moment in the world of giving!

Volunteering: Offering your time and skills is a fantastic way to make a difference without straining your wallet. Plus, it's a fulfilling experience that can provide valuable perspective – it's like getting a soul massage!

Planned Giving: This involves incorporating giving into your estate or financial plans. You can donate generously and reap potential tax benefits, all while preserving your current financial stability.

Donor-Advised Funds: By contributing to a donor-advised fund, you can get an immediate tax benefit and then recommend grants to charities over time.

Sustainable Investing: Also known as socially responsible investing, this approach involves investing in companies that align with your values, allowing your investments to make a positive impact.

As you can see, making a difference without sacrificing financial stability isn't just possible; it's an exciting adventure. So, get ready to embark on this journey of meaningful giving and savvy finance. Onward, my benevolent budgeters!

# 10.4: Case Studies: Philanthropy and Financial Health

We're about to jet off on a journey through the world of philanthropy and personal finance, visiting some folks who've discovered the secret sauce to mixing generous giving with financial stability.

First, meet Carlos, a middle-school teacher with a heart for the environment. He started by allocating a small portion of his income to charities focused on conservation. Then he went a step further and invested in environmentally friendly companies, marrying his passion for Mother Nature with his financial goals. The result? A healthy portfolio that's as green as a spring meadow!

Next, we visit Jenny, a successful entrepreneur. She used a donor-advised fund to manage her charitable giving, gaining tax benefits while systematically supporting the causes she cared about. Plus, she set up a scholarship fund at her alma mater as part of her estate plan, ensuring her wealth would continue to impact future generations. Talk about a master class in strategic giving!

Last but not least, let's drop in on Sam and Rita, a couple passionate about community service. They made volunteering a cornerstone of their giving, offering their skills to local nonprofits. But they didn't stop there. They also made use of their employer's donation matching program to double their monetary impact without doubling their personal expense. A high-flying double act if there ever was one!

These stories spotlight the incredible possibilities of integrating philanthropy into personal finance. Whether you're a teacher, a business owner, or an ordinary person with a heart for giving, there are ways to make a difference without sacrificing your financial stability. Now, isn't that a satisfying blend? Until the next tale, keep those giving gears in motion!

# Chapter 11

## 11.1: Reflecting on Your Financial Journey

The great philosopher Socrates once said, "An unexamined life is not worth living." Now, whether or not you agree with Socrates on the existential plane, the guy was definitely onto something when it comes to finances. An unexamined financial journey is like wandering through a labyrinth without a map. You might reach the end eventually, but you'll probably meet a Minotaur or two along the way.

Reflection is like that moment you sit down after a hike, look back at the trail you've traversed, and say, "Wow, did I really do that?" It's the moment when you take stock of where you've been, acknowledge your progress, celebrate your victories, and learn from your mistakes.

Maybe you've conquered your debt mountain, or perhaps you're just starting to chip away at it. Perhaps you've grown a lush savings garden, or maybe you're still planting the seeds. You might have an investment portfolio that would make Wall Street green with envy, or maybe you're learning how to pick your first stocks.

Whatever your journey has looked like so far, it's uniquely yours, with its own challenges and triumphs. Reflection is an opportunity to appreciate how far you've come and recommit to the journey ahead.

## 11.2: Consistently Reinforcing Your Money Habits

Just as a bodybuilder needs to consistently pump iron to maintain those bulging biceps, you, my friend, need to consistently reinforce your money habits to keep your financial muscles in top form. Consistency is the magic ingredient that transforms a wishful thinker into a goal crusher!

First things first, keep that budgeting ball rolling. Your budget isn't a "set it and forget it" crockpot recipe. It's a living, breathing entity that needs regular check-ins. Make it a habit to review and adjust your budget based on your changing needs and goals.

Next up, savings. Remember, saving isn't a sprint; it's a marathon. You don't need to stash away half your income in one go (unless you're secretly a superhero, in which case, carry on). Even a small, consistent amount can grow into a substantial nest egg over time.

When it comes to investing, patience and regularity are your allies. Consistently contributing to your investment accounts, even during market lows, can pay off in the long run. It's like feeding a pet – regular, balanced meals are better than one big feast!

Debt repayment is another area that thrives on consistency. Regular payments, even if they're small, can whittle down debt more effectively than sporadic lump sums.

And let's not forget about giving. Regular donations, volunteering, or even acts of kindness can make a world of difference without causing a financial strain.

Finally, take time regularly to review your financial plan. Are your goals still the same? Do you need to adjust your strategies? Regular check-ins will ensure that your plan stays relevant and effective.

Consistency is key! Keep flexing those financial muscles, and you'll be amazed at the strength you'll build. Now, go forth and conquer, you financial gladiator, you!

# 11.3: Building Resilience in Your Financial Life

Firstly, think of an emergency fund as your financial safety net. This is a stash of money set aside to cover life's "Oh Schnitzel!" moments, like sudden medical expenses or a job loss. An ideal emergency fund could cover three to six months' worth of living expenses. It's the superhero's secret lair, always there when you need to make a quick escape.

Secondly, diversification is your financial resilience's best friend. It's like having an all-you-can-eat buffet of investments: if one dish turns out to be less tasty, you've got a whole spread of other options to fill your plate.

Thirdly, insurance. Yep, it's like the spinach to your financial Popeye. It might not be your favorite thing, but boy, can it power you up when life lands a punch. Health, life, auto, home - insurance can protect you from financial blows that could otherwise knock you off your feet.

Next up, continuous learning. Financial resilience is about adapting to changes, and knowledge is your guide. Stay informed about financial trends, learn new strategies, and keep fine-tuning your financial acumen.

Finally, remember the golden rule of resilience: keep your cool. Financial downturns, market volatility, unexpected expenses - these can cause a lot of stress. But remember, you're a financial superhero! With your emergency fund, diversified investments, insurance, and knowledge, you've got what it takes to weather the storm.

So, go ahead, put on that cape of financial resilience, and face the world of finance with a fearless smile. You've got this!

# 11.4: Case Studies: Long-Term Financial Success

This time, we'll be exploring the thrilling tales of individuals who have achieved long-term financial success. Trust me, it's more exhilarating than a roller-coaster ride, with none of the stomach-churning loops!

Meet Jamie, who started his career at an entry-level job, earning just above minimum wage. He embraced the power of budgeting and saving, putting aside even small amounts consistently. He also ventured into the world of investing, starting small and learning along the way. Fast forward to today, Jamie is comfortably retired, proving that regular small steps can indeed lead to big leaps!

Now, let's turn to Priya, a single mother who found herself in a pool of debt after a sudden divorce. Rather than being overwhelmed, Priya channeled her energy into creating a robust debt repayment plan. She also picked up freelance work to diversify her income. With discipline and resilience, Priya not only cleared her debts but also built a solid financial foundation for her and her daughter.

Finally, there's Ben, a serial entrepreneur. His journey is a powerful testament to the importance of learning from failure. After his first two ventures failed, Ben picked himself up and used the lessons he had learned to launch a successful business. He emphasized the value of a good financial cushion, which provided him with the resilience to weather the early storms of entrepreneurship.

These stories offer glimpses of what long-term financial success can look like. They're as diverse as a bag of jelly beans, each with its unique flavor and color, but they all share the common thread of discipline, resilience, and a commitment to financial health. Whether you're a regular employee, a single parent, or an ambitious entrepreneur, remember, long-term financial success is a journey, not a sprint. Enjoy the ride!

# Chapter 12

## 12.1: The Lifelong Journey of Financial Success

Financial success doesn't have a finish line where you can dust off your hands and say, "Well, that's done!" Instead, it evolves with you, transforming as your life changes. Maybe you're hustling through your early career years, or navigating the financial labyrinth of raising a family, or perhaps even sailing towards the horizon of retirement.

But in every phase, financial success looks a little different, and that's okay. What matters is that you keep journeying, keep exploring, and most importantly, keep learning.

Remember, there's no 'one-size-fits-all' roadmap to financial success. Your journey is yours alone, complete with its unique landscapes and landmarks. So, buckle up, adjust your mirrors, and let's hit the road to financial success, one mile at a time!

## 12.2: Taking the Next Steps

As we descend the last chapter of this financial trek, you might be itching to ask, "Alright, we've learned a ton, but what now? What's the next step?" Well, the answer is simpler than you might think: just start!

First, embrace the mindset shift. Begin seeing money not as a means to an end but as a tool that empowers you to live the life you want. This change in perspective is the first, and arguably the most crucial, step towards financial success.

Next, make budgeting your new best friend. If you haven't already, sketch a realistic budget that caters to your lifestyle and goals. Remember, a budget isn't a cage; it's a framework that helps you manage your money effectively.

Don't forget to sprinkle the saving habit into your daily routine. Whether it's a penny or a dollar, every bit you save is a step closer to your financial goals.

Then, dip your toes in the investment pool. Start small if you must, but start nonetheless. Remember, in the world of investing, time can be a more powerful ally than money.

Debt management, income diversification, retirement planning, estate planning, giving back - these are all vital chapters in your financial story. Approach them one at a time, and remember, progress, not perfection, is the goal.

Lastly, keep learning. Your financial education doesn't stop here. Stay curious, keep exploring, and remember, every question you ask is a step closer to financial wisdom.

So there you have it. The next steps towards your financial success. Ready to take the leap? Of course, you are! Let's dive right in!

# 12.3: Staying Inspired and Motivated

Maintaining your financial health, much like physical fitness, requires ongoing effort and discipline. Picture it like a marathon, not a sprint, and every so often, even the most determined marathon runner could use a water break and a cheering squad.

To keep your enthusiasm levels topped up, find what motivates you. Maybe it's the dream of a beach house, the freedom to switch careers, or the desire to give your children a better start in life. Keep that picture in your mind, just like a trophy at the end of the marathon.

Next, don't forget to celebrate your victories, big and small. Paid off a debt? Hooray! Reached a saving milestone? That calls for a celebration! Managed to stick to your budget for a whole month? Time for a happy dance! These milestones are not just wins; they're reminders that you're making progress, and progress is always worth celebrating.

Moreover, create a supportive network around you. They say it takes a village to raise a child, and it might just take a community to achieve financial success. This could be a group of friends committed to financial health, a mentor who guides you, or even online communities. They can offer advice, share their experiences, and give you that boost when the going gets tough.

And finally, remain patient. There will be bumps along the road, and that's okay. Remember, it's a marathon, not a sprint. Financial success takes time to build, so keep running the race, one step at a time. With a dash of perseverance and a pinch of patience, you've got the perfect recipe to stay inspired and motivated on your financial journey.

# 12.4: Final Thoughts and Encouragements

Alright, we've crossed the bridges, conquered the mountains, and navigated the winding roads of our financial expedition. As we draw the curtains on this narrative, I hope you're stepping away with a head full of knowledge, a heart full of courage, and a pocket full of, well, hopefully more money.

Financial success is not a fairy tale where a magic wand turns pumpkins into riches. No, it's a story of determination, discipline, and smart decisions. It's the tale of individuals who, like you, embarked on a journey with the goal of making their money work for them.

As you continue your journey beyond these pages, remember to embrace change. The world of finance is as dynamic as a salsa dancer, always in motion. So, keep your dancing shoes on, and don't be afraid to sway with the changing rhythms of the financial world.

Remain curious, for knowledge is the compass that will guide you on your journey. Keep asking questions, keep learning, and keep growing.

And most importantly, don't lose sight of why you embarked on this journey. Behind all the talk of money, budgets, and investments, lies the essence of financial success: the freedom to live the life you want, the ability to weather life's storms, and the opportunity to create a positive impact in your world.

So, as we part ways, I encourage you to take the helm of your financial ship and chart a course towards success. Be brave, be wise, and most importantly, enjoy the journey. For in the grand adventure of financial success, the journey is just as important, if not more, as the destination.

Until our next financial adventure, keep the 'Money Habit' alive. Happy journeying!

9 798852 760814